W9-CIR-314

THE BLACKFOOT

by Elizabeth Hahn

Illustrated by Katherine Ace

ROURKE PUBLICATIONS, INC.

VERO BEACH, FLORIDA 32964

CONTENTS

Library of Congress Cataloging-in-Publication Data

Hahn, Elizabeth, 1942-
   The Blackfoot / by Elizabeth Hahn; illustrated by Katherine Ace.
     p.   cm. —(Native American people)
   Includes index.
   Summary: Describes the history, way of life, and current status of the Blackfoot Indians.
     1. Siksika Indians—Juvenile literature. [1. Siksika Indians. 2. Indians of North America.] I. Ace, Katherine, ill. II. Title. III. Series.
E99.S4H24 1992   91-48096
   ISBN 0-86625-395-5   CIP
                                 AC

INTRODUCTION

People are sometimes confused about the names, Blackfoot and Blackfeet. Many think that Blackfeet is just the plural of Blackfoot. This is not true. There are, indeed, two different tribes of Native Americans. The Blackfeet are a small Sioux tribe from the Dakota territory. The Blackfoot, descendants of a large and powerful Algonquian tribe, are located in Montana and Canada.

Historians do not know for certain how the Blackfoot got their name. Some people say there is a legend about how the Blackfoots' ancestors walked through the aftermath of a prairie fire for so many days that their moccasins turned black. Others believe that early members of the tribe painted their moccasins black, earning them the name. Today, no evidence remains of black moccasins, nor can any Blackfoot verify the accuracy of the ancient legend, so the origin of the name remains a mystery.

The Blackfoot migrated west from the great forestlands of the Northeast. Researchers know this because the Blackfoot language is Algonquian, like that of their northeastern ancestors. The Blackfoot traveled all the way to the foothills of the Rocky Mountains, which provided an excellent natural boundary to the Blackfoot territory. The territory filled the northwest corner of the Great Plains in what today is the state of Montana. It also extended into adjacent parts of the province of Alberta, Canada.

The Blackfoot were a nomadic people whose lives centered around hunting buffalo. They followed the great herds across the vast plains grasslands. The buffalo supplied all the Blackfoots' needs: food, shelter, clothing, and tools.

By 1830, the Blackfoot were at the height of their power. Unlike many other Native American tribes, the Blackfoot never used their strength to enter a formal war against the United States. Part of this is due to the fact that a great portion of Blackfoot lands lay in Canada, so the westward expansion of the United States did not affect them as severely as it did other tribes.

If the Blackfoot were strong enough to fend off just about any enemy, there was one that they were not able to subdue: smallpox, the white people's disease. Four different smallpox epidemics in the 19th century devastated the Blackfoot population.

At the same time, the number of buffalo was getting ever smaller. White hunters were killing them by the thousands. By 1883, the Blackfoot were returning empty-handed from their hunts. They then began trading furs with the white people in exchange for supplies and food, but still the tribe was starving. Some members became so desperate that they took to raiding and stealing from white settlements. The U.S. Army was called in to bring order to the territory. In 1869, however, soldiers mistakenly attacked a peaceful Blackfoot camp and killed every man, woman, and child.

Between the disorder and the disease, the Blackfoots' strength and spirit were all but completely broken. Some of the survivors moved across the border into Canada, and the others agreed to live peacefully on the small parcel of reservation land the U.S. government set aside for them in Montana. There many of them remain today, descendants of the once-powerful, once-numerous Blackfoot nation.

The BLACKFOOT

CANADA

← The
Blackfoot

U.S.A.

MEXICO

Way of Life

THE Blackfoot depended on the buffalo for their very existence, and they believed that the migrations of the great herds were directed by the gods. At one time, more than 60 million buffalo roamed the Great Plains. To make hunting easy, the Blackfoot had few possessions, and everything they owned had to be portable—even their houses. Called tipis, these tent-like houses were made from long wooden poles and buffalo-skin coverings.

The tipi was a perfect house for these wanderers. It was sturdy enough to withstand both the strong summer winds and the blinding winter snowstorms that blew across the Plains. At the same time, it was light enough for the women to set up and break down easily at each new campsite. Collapsed, the tipi served another purpose: It formed a kind of sled called a *travois* (trav-WAH).

To make the travois, two of the tipi's main poles were tied to the shoulders of a dog or horse, and the other ends of the poles were left to drag along the ground. The remaining poles and the buffalo-skin tipi covering were loaded on top of the sled. Then, the Blackfoots' few belongings were piled on top of the buffalo skins. At the next campsite, the women could easily detach the travois from the animals' shoulders and set up the tents.

During the hot summer months, the women rolled the tipi's buffalo covering up a few feet from the ground to let the breezes cool the inside of the tent. In the bitter cold of the winter months, the covering was pegged securely to the ground. Then extra buffalo skins were hung inside the tipi for more insulation against the cold. The women maintained a fire in the center of the tipi to cook and to keep the tipi warm.

As the women set up camp, the men went out into the grasslands to hunt the buffalo. Before they had horses, the Blackfoot tracked the buffalo on foot and killed them in several different ways. The easiest way was to drive the buffalo over a blind cliff—a cliff that the Blackfoot could see but the buffalo could not. To do this, the hunters crept up close on the downwind side of the herd so that

Frightened buffalo stampede over a cliff in this diorama of Two Medicine River.

6

the animals did not pick up their human scent. On a predetermined signal, the men shouted and waved flaming torches to scare the buffalo. The frightened animals stampeded, racing in a blind panic right over the cliff and killing themselves in the fall. The blind cliffs proved to be such a successful hunting tactic that the Blackfoot renamed them "buffalo jumps."

Another Blackfoot hunting technique was for the men to cover themselves with buffalo skins and horns so that they could get close to the animals without frightening them. Then the hunters speared the buffalo with lances or shot them with bows and arrows.

The introduction of the horse to Blackfoot life in the 18th century dramatically changed the tribe's hunting tactics. Now the hunters could venture much farther from camp in search of buffalo herds, and the horses could carry much more meat and skins back to camp. The hunt itself became more exciting as the men rode their horses at a full gallop into the running herds.

Riding bareback and grasping his horse with only his legs so as to free his hands, the hunter would shoot an arrow deep into the buffalo. Immediately after such a daring kill, the hunter leaped down from his horse and cut out the heart of the buffalo, which he ate raw. To the Blackfoot, a good hunt was cause for immediate celebration, and though it may seem unappetizing to us, a buffalo's heart was considered a special treat to eat by the Blackfoot. Hunters also drank the buffalo's blood. It was an honor for a brave to offer and share the heart and blood of his kill with another hunter.

Two women begin butchering a newly killed buffalo.

Buffalo Supplies

Blackfoot men did the buffalo hunting, but it was the women who actually butchered the animals. They cut some meat up for roasts, but most of it was cut into thin strips and hung on racks to dry in the sun. Dried, this meat was called jerky, and it was good to eat even months after the hunt. The women also pounded some of the meat into small pieces and mixed it with fat and berries to make a nutritious food called *pemmican*. Because the Blackfoot had no grains to make cereal or bread, they used pemmican as a staple in their diet in the same way that other tribes used cereal or bread. Pemmican could be stored in the camp for long periods of time, and the braves always carried some in their packs when they were away from camp.

Buffalo skins had many different uses. Skins taken in the late fall and winter were the furriest, so they were used to make warm buffalo robes or blankets. In the winter, the buffalo robes were hung as a lining inside the tipis for extra insulation from the cold. They were also used as bed coverings inside the tipi. Then, too, the robe was worn as clothing, hair-side out in the summer and hair-side in during the winter for warmth. The skin side of the robe was often decorated. It could be painted with geometric designs or with picture art describing the owner's exploits. Sometimes the skins were also decorated with beautiful quillwork—designs made from colored porcupine quills that the women sewed onto buffalo robes and other garments.

Skins taken during the spring and summer months were scraped clean by the women and made into rawhide.

Rawhide had numerous uses. Some was made into hunting shields, covers for drums, or *parfleches* (par-FLESH), leather storage pouches. Rawhide was also sewn together to make tipi coverings. It took from 6 to 20 hides to cover a tipi. Thread to sew the hides together was made from the tendons that stretch along buffalos' legs.

The Blackfoot stretched strips of rawhide to form a kind of rope. This was used to make harnesses and bridles for their horses, and tools for hunting and warfare. The rawhide strips served as thongs to attach stone heads to war clubs, stone points to wooden shafts to make arrows, and flint spearheads to larger shafts to make lances. The thongs were tied on wet. As the rawhide dried, it shrank to make an extremely tight bond.

Other pieces of rawhide were stretched and staked out on the ground where they were left to dry to form a kind of canvas for paintings. Blackfoot artists might cover these canvases with colorful designs or with pictures that told a story, such as an old tribal legend or a recent adventure of a great warrior.

Buffalo horns and bones, too, had many uses. They were made into tools, spoons, bowls, needles, paint brushes, hair ornaments, and drinking cups. Even the buffalo's hair was useful. It was woven into rope or rolled into balls for games. Loose, it was used to stuff pillows and cradleboards, small frameworks that mothers wore on their backs to carry their babies. And buffalo hair was used to line moccasins to keep feet warm and dry in winter. Even buffalo manure was used. Known as "buffalo chips," the dried manure provided fuel for Blackfoot campfires.

Last, but far from least, the rawhide was used to make clothing for the Blackfoot. The women softened the rawhide skins that were to be made into clothing by rubbing the skins with a mixture of buffalo brains and fat. Next they spread the skins on the ground and marked the appropriate shape on them with a piece of charcoal or a sharp stick that made an indentation in the skins. Then the women cut and sewed the pieces into leggings, shirts, dresses, and moccasins, using tendons for thread.

Clothing

Everyday Blackfoot clothing, made from the softened buffalo skins, was plain and simple. The men wore moccasins and leggings that covered their legs from their hips down to their ankles. These leggings were attached to a leather waist belt by rawhide strips. The outfit was topped by a long shirt that reached down to the thighs or by a buffalo robe. When they went to war or to hunt, the men usually wore just a pair of sturdy moccasins and a leather breechclout. The breechclout, also known as a breechcloth, was made of two pieces of rawhide attached to a leather waist belt.

During the winter, the men wore fur-lined moccasins and added furry buffalo robes to their shirts and leggings. They also wore fur headbands or hats. The headbands were actually a strip of buffalo hide or wolf skin about nine inches wide. The men tied these around their heads and ears.

Their hats were made of the fur of animals such as the wolf, badger, or coyote, or from the skins of large birds such as ravens and hawks. Hats created from small animals were often made with the animal's ears still attached, so that the men looked more animal-like than human when they bundled up against the winter cold. They never wore mittens or any other covering on their hands.

The women, like the men, wore buffalo-skin leggings and moccasins. Instead of shirts, they wore long leather dresses tied around the waist with a rawhide belt. Sometimes they decorated their dresses with fringe or quillwork. In the winter, they, too, wrapped themselves in warm buffalo robes and wore fur-lined moccasins.

Men's ceremonial clothes were decorated with fringe and elaborate quillwork, and included special shirts that were made from the skin of the bighorn sheep. These skins were a beautiful white color. Decorated with colored quillwork or unusual furs such as white ermine, these shirts looked quite regal. Because these shirts were so elaborately decorated, they could never be washed. When they became dirty, the owner simply painted them a reddish-brown color.

Hair care was important to the Blackfoot because they were particularly attentive to their appearance. The women parted their hair in the middle and wore two long braids, or let their hair hang loose with a headband around their forehead. The men were even more particular about their hair than the women. Young braves wore their hair loose, but they cut an unusual, long, squared-off bang that hung down over their foreheads between their eyes to the tip of their nose. Older men did not wear bangs. Instead, they twisted their long hair into a knot that they wore on their forehead. Some of these knots were so large that they stuck out seven or eight inches from their heads.

Both men and women washed and brushed their hair carefully, using hairbrushes made from porcupine tails. Sometimes they greased their hair with buffalo fat to slick it down and give it added sheen.

Chief Mountain wearing his fringed buckskin shirt, feather hair ornaments, and beads.

A medicine man wears the skin of a yellow bear and other animals in order to take on their qualities.

Tribal Societies

The Blackfoot were organized into a system of three different kinds of societies: warrior societies, a religious society, and women's societies. Each society had its origin in an ancient legend that had come to a tribe member in a vision or a dream. The Blackfoot believed that in the earliest days of the tribe, special members of the tribe had such visions or dreams, in which they met beings considered to be supernatural and acting as messengers of the gods. These divine messengers were believed to have instructed the tribal representative on how to form a particular society for the tribe. The messenger also dictated rules about how the society should be formed, what customs and traditions were to be observed, and what ceremonial regalia was to be used in order to maintain the proper respect for the gods.

Membership in a society was by invitation. The leaders decided who they would ask to join. The warrior societies were age-graded, meaning that boys and young men were invited to join different levels at specific ages. All other Blackfoot societies were not age-graded. That is, when a young person reached adulthood, only then was he or she invited to join the society. Full adult responsibilities would be assumed immediately. Once a Blackfoot joined a society, he or she usually remained in it for life.

The warrior societies were the largest and strongest among the Blackfoot. Being age-graded, they delegated responsibilities according to a member's age. The youngest members assumed small tasks, and as the young boys grew, they moved up to more advanced responsibilities. Reaching adulthood, they then assumed the society's full adult responsibilities. Even the names of the groups within the warrior societies indicate how the different age levels were regarded. The young Doves or Mosquitoes, for example, did not have the same tasks as the older Braves, Brave Dogs, Soldiers, or Bulls.

The warrior society's responsibilities included maintaining order in the camp, monitoring the location of buffalo herds and organizing hunting parties, guarding the camp against enemy attacks, and planning and leading war parties.

The religious society consisted of older men who had fulfilled their military obligations and now served as holy men and counselors for the tribe. They organized all tribal ceremonies, preserved the tribe's religious heritage and traditions, and helped members interpret their dreams and visions.

The women's societies had a variety of responsibilities. Some helped perform rituals related to the buffalo in ceremonies dedicated to fruitful hunts. Others assisted in ceremonies held to ask for the rebirth of the animals killed during the hunt so that there would always be plenty of game. Still other women's societies functioned as craft guilds. In them, groups of women participated in tribal arts such as quillwork. Women's war societies also existed. Consisting of only a few women, the members followed the men to war to cook for them or, in rare instances, to fight with them.

Each Blackfoot society was structured so that everyone in it performed a valuable role in tribal life. The society system was a well-ordered system that organized the various aspects of Blackfoot life.

Weasel Tail, also known as Medicine Pipe Man.

A Blackfoot family stands next to its tipi.

Ceremonial Regalia and Rituals

All ceremonial regalia and ritual information, because it was believed to be provided by the gods, was considered holy. Thus, each part of the regalia and rituals served not only to identify a society. Even more important, it served to remind its members that their society's power and knowledge had come directly from the gods and that those gods demanded respect.

Each society had special regalia. Regalia is the combination of emblems, decorations, clothing, and other objects that are the signs or symbols of a group or an important person. The regalia of each Blackfoot society included a variety of items. The regalia of the religious society included peace pipes, various relics that were considered sacred gifts of the gods, and special songs and chants. The regalia of the warrior societies, however, were uniquely dramatic. They included a society sash and staff. The sash was a long piece of rawhide that was decorated with paintings, quillwork, feathers, and bits of animal fur, all of which were arranged to tell a story about the society or its protecting god.

Ah-kay-ee-pix-en, dressed in a goat skin.

In-ne-o-cose, Iron Horse, with his medicine bag.

Only the bravest members of the warrior societies were entitled to wear the sacred sash. They had to prove their bravery by taking the sash into battle, tying it around their waists, and staking the other end into the ground. The object was for a warrior to stand his ground in the midst of the battle. Standing his ground was believed to be a test of his faith in the gods who had empowered him. A warrior would fight till death, if necessary, rather than pull up the sash and admit defeat.

The staff of warrior societies was a spear or lance that was used only for battle coups. A coup was the act of touching an enemy, but not killing him. The object was only to demonstrate bravery, not to fell an enemy. Like the sash, the warrior's staff was lavishly decorated. Animal skins were wrapped around the staff. Then, feathers, soft down from swans, hair locks, and enemy scalps were added to make the staff a stronger symbol of power. One had to be a leader of the warrior society to carry the staff into battle.

Before a warrior carried the regalia into battle, he had to perform certain preparatory rituals. These, too, had been prescribed by the gods. First, the warrior had to purify himself in a sweat lodge, a small, dome-like structure built of willow branches and covered with buffalo skins. Sweet grass was spread on the floor of the lodge and a fire was built in the center of the structure to heat a pile of rocks. When the rocks got hot enough, the warrior sweated profusely. The sweat was supposed to carry any bad elements out of his body. Then, water was poured on the hot stones, creating clouds of steam that enveloped the warrior, a further means of purifying his body.

Pe-toh-pee-kiss, also called Eagle Ribs, was a Blackfoot warrior.

Next, the warrior painted his body, but it was not just simple decoration. The painting was intended to help transform the warrior into the creature he was representing for the gods and his society. If, for example, he was to fight like a bear, the warrior painted himself like a bear. Then, the warrior painted his horse with society symbols that were intended to bring special powers to the horse.

All of this regalia and ritual was for the warrior who already was a member of a society. Other warriors, not yet members of a society, undertook a ritual process called a vision quest. Its purpose was to enable the man to communicate with the gods for insight and understanding about his future.

15

The Vision Quest

The Blackfoot people took their religion seriously. They believed that everything was created by the gods, and furthermore, that everything had not only a life of its own on Earth, but also an on-going relationship with the gods. Everything—plants, animals, rocks, trees, water, wind, and human beings—contained life and was on Earth to serve the gods. The Blackfoot believed that they could learn from all different forms of life. Rocks, for example, because of their permanent, enduring quality, taught the Blackfoot about the eternal nature of the gods. Turtles, because they lived for many years, taught them about long life. Animals such as the wolf or bear, and birds such as the eagle, also offered lessons to the Blackfoot. These animals were blessed with great strength, courage, and fighting skills, qualities the Blackfoot believed they could acquire if they captured the spirit of the bird or animal.

The way in which the Blackfoot captured the spirit of these animals was

through a ritual called a vision quest. This ritual marked a rite of passage—the transition from childhood to adulthood—for Blackfoot men. Women rarely went on such a quest. In the Blackfoot culture, it was not considered necessary or appropriate for a woman to undertake a vision quest. Women's roles were limited to caring for their families and households.

A young man went through elaborate preparations for his quest. First he had to seek the council of tribal leaders and members of the religious society. These elders instructed the young man on how to proceed. Then the young Blackfoot fasted and underwent a sweat-lodge purification ritual, followed by a bath, prayers, and incense burning. Next, the young man was painted with white clay to symbolize his purity. Then, just before he embarked on a journey to some distant, solitary place, the men of the religious society organized a Ghost Dance on his behalf. The dance was performed to seek protection for the young man from fearful night spirits or ghosts that he might encounter on his nights alone in the wilderness.

After all of the preparations were completed, the young man walked many miles from his camp to find an isolated spot in the wilderness. There he sat for one to four days and nights, praying to the gods for a vision to come. As he waited for the vision, he opened his mind to receive it. In the vision, any one of the gods' creatures—a bird, an animal, a rock, or even an herb—might come and speak to the young man about his future. Whoever or whatever appeared to the young man would be his helper-guide throughout life. The helper-guide communicated to the young man what things he needed—an eagle's feather or a bear's tooth, for example—in order to become more like the guide. In all his future life, the young man would practice being like an eagle or a bear—or whatever his guide was—to insure harmony with the gods and success in living.

After receiving a vision, the young man returned to camp where the men of the religious society helped interpret the meaning of his vision. From that day on, the young man accepted the full responsibilities of an adult within the tribe.

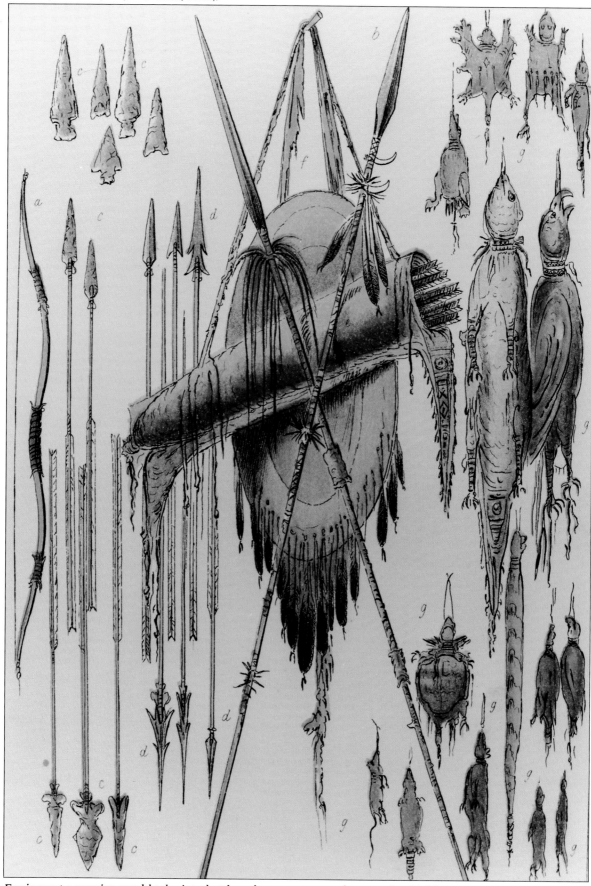

Equipment a warrior would take into battle — lances, arrows, a bow, and a shield.

Warrior on horseback.
(Photo courtesy of Oregon Historical Society)

The Importance of the Horse

Historians generally believe that the horse became a part of Blackfoot life as early as the 1700s. The animals were first introduced to Native Americans in the Southern Plains by the Spanish explorer, Coronado, around 1530. Horses gradually made their way north through intertribal trading or stealing. The Blackfoot first called the horse *ponokamita*, or "elk dog." Horses made the Blackfoot much more mobile, enlarged the area in which they could hunt, and made them feared warriors.

The Blackfoot began to raise large herds of horses, and soon measured their wealth by the size of their herds. Sometimes, part of this wealth was used to buy a bride. The number of horses a man gave his bride's father was a measure both of his love for his bride and of the wealth he was bringing to the marriage. Some of the more powerful Blackfoot had herds that numbered in the thousands.

Blackfoot boys began to ride horses as soon as they were able to walk and they became some of the finest horsemen among the Plains tribes. The braves always rode bareback. Riding in the heat of battle, they swung themselves over onto one side of their galloping horse. Then the warrior hooked one leg over the back of the horse and wrapped the other around the horse's stomach. With his arms holding onto the horse's neck, the warrior actually rode the horse's side where the enemy could not see or easily wound him. The ingenious, side-riding horsemen could even hold onto their horses with only their legs so that their arms were free to shoot arrows either under or over the horse's neck.

The Blackfoot acquired horses in several different ways: stealing them from their enemies; capturing wild horses; and breeding them. They quickly learned how to match their best horses to produce stronger and faster ones.

The horse was so important to the Blackfoot that a warrior's favorite horse was killed at the warrior's funeral. That way, the horse could accompany his master into the spirit world.

Brown Weasel: Blackfoot Woman Warrior

Brown Weasel was an unusual girl. The oldest of four children, she was the daughter of a famous Blackfoot warrior. Early on she was bored with the sewing, cooking, rawhide tanning, and childcare lessons taught to her by her mother and aunts. Believing that her brothers had a much more exciting life, she asked her father to teach her how to ride horses and shoot a bow and arrow. Her father knew it was an out-of-the-ordinary request, but he loved his brave daughter, so he agreed. Soon Brown Weasel rode as well as any boy in the camp, and she was so expert with a bow and arrow that her father often let her accompany him on buffalo hunts.

Many of the other warriors were unhappy about Brown Weasel, thinking that a girl did not belong in their hunting parties. One day Brown Weasel proved her skill and courage to everyone. Riding after the buffalo, the Blackfoot hunting party was attacked by a band of enemy warriors. They shot Brown Weasel's father's horse out from under him, leaving him helpless on foot. Without a moment's hesitation, Brown Weasel turned her horse and galloped directly into the enemy forces to rescue her father. With arrows flying all around her, she grasped her pony's neck and slid over onto its side while it galloped at full speed. Then she thrust out her arm for her father to grasp, enabling him to swing himself up onto her pony right behind her.

It was an amazing rescue. Only the most courageous of warriors ever attempted to rescue a brave stranded on foot amongst the enemy. When Brown Weasel and her father returned to their camp, there was a great celebration, fitting tribute to the young girl's skill and courage.

Unfortunately, not long after, Brown Weasel's father was killed in another battle, and her mother died of heartbreak after learning of her husband's death. Brown Weasel struggled to decide how best to care for her younger brothers and sisters. She decided to assume her father's warrior role. To help her achieve her goal, she invited an old widow to live with her family to do all the household work. Everyone in her village was not as eager as Brown Weasel was about her plans. Other members of the tribe may have recognized Brown Weasel's bravery during the buffalo hunts, but it was a whole other thing for them to accept her as a warrior.

At first, the chief did not let Brown Weasel join the war parties. She followed them anyway. When the warriors discovered her, they tried to send her back to camp, but Brown Weasel refused. Reluctantly they at last let her go along— and a wise move that turned out to be. For soon she again proved her worth in action. A small Blackfoot war party set out to retrieve some horses that had been stolen by enemy Crow tribesmen. At night, the Blackfoot slipped into the Crow camp and recaptured all of the stolen horses. Brown Weasel took 11 back by herself, but that was just a small part of what was to be for Brown Weasel.

On the way back to their camp, the Blackfoot stopped one night to rest. Brown Weasel was on guard when she saw two Crow warriors sneaking up to the Blackfoot campsite. First she ran to the herd of horses to make sure their ropes were tied securely. The Crow warriors saw her but concluded they had nothing to fear because she was a woman. That was their big mistake.

Brown Weasel grabbed her rifle and shot one of the Crow as he tried to cut the horses free from their ropes. Knowing she did not have time to reload her own gun, Brown Weasel grabbed the gun from the Crow she had shot and fired at the other Crow who by then was frantically trying to get out of the Blackfoot campsite. Brown Weasel missed, but the commotion awakened the rest of the Blackfoot, enabling another warrior to kill the remaining Crow.

Again, Brown Weasel's people were proud of her. Though it had been her first

war party, Brown Weasel had not only retrieved 11 horses, she also had killed an enemy and captured his gun and horse. The chief and other tribal leaders decided that Brown Weasel was, indeed, a special young woman. They would allow her to undertake a vision quest, a rare privilege for a young Blackfoot girl.

After consulting with the council of tribal leaders and the men of the religious society, Brown Weasel performed the necessary preparatory rituals, then went by herself into the wilderness for four days. There she had a powerful vision that instructed her to dedicate her life to the sun and to her people. Upon returning to her village, Brown Weasel changed her dress for a warrior's clothing and a rawhide shield. Then at a big summer encampment of many different Blackfoot tribes, Brown Weasel was asked to stand and tell about her brave deeds. The other warriors whooped and cheered, and the chief gave Brown Weasel a new name to reflect her courage and abilities. From that day forward she would be known as Running Eagle.

Running Eagle fought bravely for many years until she was killed in a battle against warriors of the enemy Flathead tribe. The Blackfoot brought her body home and gave her a great warrior's funeral. The story of their great woman warrior has been kept alive by many generations of Blackfoot.

Blackfoot Art

The Blackfoot have always been especially talented craft artists, excelling in decorative quillwork and painting. They painted and decorated not only their clothes, but also their parfleches, shields, drumheads, and most spectacular of all, their tipis.

Winters in the Northern Plains territory of the Blackfoot were long and severe. Howling winds and persistent storms blanketed the area with deep snow. Temperatures could fall to 40 degrees below zero. In November, after a final fall hunt to lay in stores of meat, the Blackfoot moved their camps to valleys in the foothills of the Rocky Mountains where they might find some shelter from the constant, cold, and penetrating wind. From late November until early May, they kept their tipis snug and dry, and rarely went outside except to gather more fuel for the fire. They passed the days and long nights telling stories and making and decorating new clothing, ceremonial

regalia, hunting gear, cradleboards for babies, and toys for the children.

While the women did all the sewing of new clothes, both men and women painted them. Most often the women painted symbolic geometric designs, while the men painted realistic animal and human figures. To protect themselves in battle, the men painted their war shields and drum covers with pictures of the sun, moon, and stars, or the animal that was their helper-guide. Men painted their shirts and buffalo robes with picture stories about particular battles they had fought or brave deeds they had accomplished.

Men and women also painted cradleboards and small toys for their children. The Blackfoot loved children and devoted a great deal of time and attention to them. Their cradleboards could be elaborately painted and sometimes also were decorated with quillwork. Toys,

too—dolls, play tipis, and miniature travois—were specially decorated. Children were valued so greatly and were important to the tribe because it was through them that the tribe would live on. The fatality rate, especially among Blackfoot men, was high because of war and hunting accidents.

Another art form for which the Blackfoot are well known is their beautiful quillwork. Long before Native Americans secured beads from white people, the Blackfoot worked with porcupines' quills to embroider intricate and colorful designs on their clothing, moccasins, cradleboards, and ceremonial regalia. Each porcupine supplied up to 30,000 quills. When a porcupine was killed, the women pulled out the quills, sorted them by size, and washed them. Next, they dyed the quills with different colored vegetable dyes. Then they softened them by soaking them in water or by chewing them. The colorful quills were then ready to be woven or sewn onto rawhide. Some of the elaborately decorated shirts, moccasins, and other articles can be seen in museums today. Native American quillwork is widely recognized as a unique and beautiful art form.

Perhaps the most dramatic art of the Blackfoot was their tipi painting. Like most of Blackfoot life, the tipi paintings came from sacred origins. The gods were believed to give the design for the art to the tipi owner in a dream or vision quest. As often was the case, animals were considered messengers of the gods. Some animals that appeared most frequently

in a man's dreams were the buffalo, bear, elk, deer, horse, otter, and eagle. The animal in the dream communicated to the tipi owner how to paint his tipi. That way, each man in the tribe had his own design, and some were spectacular indeed. At the annual Blackfoot gatherings in Montana, it is still a breathtaking experience to see the remarkable tipis painted all over with giant buffalo or bears. One tipi painting, in which a huge bear is shown with outstretched arms, is called the "hugging bear tipi."

Even the different colored paints were considered gifts from the gods because they came from the Earth and from

A Blackfoot chief wearing elaborate dress and holding a peace pipe.

*Wun-nes-tou, White Buffalo,
the medicine man. With his
left hand he presents his
mystery drum in which are
hidden all the secrets
of his healing art.*

roots and berries, all creations of the gods. The colored clays, roots, and berries were ground into a powder and mixed with hot water and a glue compound made from buffalo fat. Artists used the porous ends of buffalo bones for brushes.

The Blackfoot painted not only their clothing and possessions. They also painted their bodies. Both men and women painted their faces, and not just for war or special ceremonies. Paint in the summer protected their faces from the sun, and in the winter it protected them from the bitter cold. Women and children painted their faces red all over. Men sometimes colored their face as well as their hands red.

Other times, men painted red only on the edge of their eyelids and in a few stripes on their cheeks. Another variation was to paint their faces yellow and their eyes red. An even more unusual fashion was to paint their cheeks red, while reserving blue for their forehead, chin, and a stripe down the nose!

"Decision," a painting by Robert F. Morgan, depicts a group of explorers trying to find their way in the vast western frontier.

A Blackfoot brave by C.M. Russell, 1898.

The Blackfoot Today

In 1806, the explorer Meriwether Lewis had what is believed to have been the first white encounter with the Blackfoot. He wrote that they seemed a strong and honest people. Beyond Lewis's encounter, there was little contact between the Blackfoot and white people. Indeed, the Blackfoots' isolation and their hostile reputation gave them a kind of immunity against white people—at least for a time.

The Blackfoot continued to thrive into the 1830s, when the tribe reached approximately 18,000 in number. After that, the Blackfoot population was ravaged by the white people's disease, smallpox, and by ever-more-aggressive white buffalo hunters. For the next 40 years, epidemics of smallpox were destined to break out every decade. The first epidemic struck in 1836, killing nearly half of the Blackfoot tribe. Subsequent epidemics in 1845, 1857, and 1869 so drastically reduced the Blackfoot population that the tribe no longer was able to ward off the white settlers who were increasingly encroaching on their lands.

White people continually expanded their buffalo hunts because the animals' skins were valuable to white merchants in the East. Some white hunters were brave enough to ask the Blackfoot to help hunt the buffalo. The Blackfoot were happy to help the white hunters because they could trade the buffalo hides for supplies such as wagons, wool cloth, beads, and most important, guns. The informal trade arrangement with the white people was outlined formally in the first treaty between white Americans and the Blackfoot in 1855. It was called Lamed Bull's Treaty after the

Ona-steh-pa-kah, Two Guns White Calf, chief and orator.

leader of all the Blackfoot chiefs at the time.

The treaty stated that the U.S. government would give the Blackfoot $20,000 annually in goods and services as well as an additional $15,000 annually for their "education and Christianization." In exchange, the Blackfoot agreed to live in perpetual peace with the white people and to limit themselves to an area approximately half the size of their former territory. They also would permit all white people to settle and travel on their lands, and would allow construction of roads, railroads, telegraph lines, military posts, and missions on their lands. Not a good treaty for the Blackfoot to begin with, the agreement was abused rather quickly as white people started sending moldy old bread, coffee, and rice for the promised "goods."

By the 1860s, white settlers moved into Blackfoot territory in ever-increasing numbers and, moreover, started cattle ranches there. The cattle competed with the buffalo for the same grasslands. As the number of buffalo diminished from the hunting that was conducted to meet the white traders' demand for skins, the

cattle overtook the Plains. The Blackfoot began to retaliate by attacking isolated white ranches and settlements. The whites called for military intervention and in 1869 the U.S. Cavalry arrived, but it mistakenly attacked a friendly Blackfoot camp.

In the ensuing battle, known as the Baker Massacre, more than 300 Blackfoot men, women, and children were killed. This brought the number of remaining Blackfoot to less than 3,000. The Blackfoot were afraid to retaliate further because they were once again fighting a smallpox epidemic and they feared that between the disease and war their entire tribe would be wiped out. They settled into a peaceful coexistence.

Still this was not enough. The white ranchers wanted even more land. As a result, President Ulysses S. Grant signed two executive orders in 1873 and 1874, which moved the southern boundary of the Blackfoot territory farther north.

The U.S. census of 1880 listed 2,200 Blackfoot. By 1883, the buffalo were gone. The winter of 1883-84 is known as "Starvation Winter" because more than 600 Blackfoot died of hunger. To survive,

Ulysses S. Grant, eighteenth President of the United States

(Photo courtesy of Historical Pictures Service)

the remaining Blackfoot desperately needed the goods and services the white people had promised in Lamed Bull's Treaty. Never upheld in good faith by the white people, nor were the treaty's terms adhered to at this time. To get help, the Blackfoot capitulated completely, agreeing to keep solely on the narrow strip of reservation land provided by the U.S. government.

In 1898, the U.S. Congress passed the Curtis Act, which abolished the rights of all tribal governments for Native Americans. The government hoped the ensuing "assimilation process" would bring all Native Americans into the culture of white America. This decision was not reversed until 1934, when Congress passed the Wheeler-Howard Act. The law allowed Native Americans to reinstitute their tribal governments, but by then there was not much left of the Blackfoot nation to reinstitute.

Some of the young Blackfoot men were drafted into military service during World War I (1914-1918) and World War II (1939-1945). This was the Blackfoots' first introduction to life off the reservation. When the wars ended, the Blackfoot soldiers did not want to return to their old, empty existence on the reservation. Some moved West to major cities in Oregon and Washington, where they could find employment opportunities.

By the 1950s and 1960s, very few Blackfoot people even knew or were studying their tribe's Algonquian language. It wasn't until the 1970s that the new generation of Blackfoot realized that they had all but completely lost their heritage. They turned to the few remaining elders to learn the stories and traditions of their culture.

Now, both white people and the Blackfoot realize how devastating the loss of yet another Native American culture would be to America's broad cultural history. Ordinary people and researchers are investigating the Blackfoots' past and rereading their myths and legends. In that way, the traditions of this once-great people will not disappear.

Today, Blackfoot tribal councils host an annual Indian Days celebration on the Montana reservation lands. During the festival, held every July, the Blackfoot build a traditional encampment of painted tipis. Ceremonies, games, contests in horsemanship, storytelling, and craft exhibits take place during the celebration. The event lasts for four days—the same amount of time as was given to the ancient vision quests. And at this modern event, too, people come away with a vision. This time it is a vision of the Blackfoots' rich cultural heritage.

Blackfoot brave painted by C.M. Russell.

Important Dates in Blackfoot History

1540	The Spanish explorer Francisco Coronado introduces the horse to Native Americans in the Southern Plains. Through intertribal trading, the horse gradually makes its way north to Blackfoot territory.
1806	The American explorer Meriwether Lewis, of the Lewis and Clark Expedition, travels through the northwest territories and encounters the isolated Blackfoot. He reports that they are a strong and honest people.
1830	Blackfoot civilization is at its height with an estimated population of more than 18,000.
1836	The first great smallpox epidemic kills close to half of the Blackfoot.
1845-1857	Disastrous smallpox epidemics again strike the Blackfoot, reducing the tribe's population to five or six thousand people.
1855	Lamed Bull's Treaty is signed. It is the first treaty between the U.S. government and the Blackfoot.
1860s	White settlers pour into Blackfoot territory in vast numbers. They begin to raise large herds of cattle, and fence in vast parts of the rich grasslands, reducing the grazing space of the buffalo.
1869	The Baker Massacre takes place in which more than 300 Blackfoot men, women, and children are mistakenly massacred by the U.S. Cavalry.
1869	Another smallpox epidemic strikes the Blackfoot, further reducing their already-small numbers.
1873-1874	U.S. President Ulysses S. Grant signs two executive orders reducing the size of Blackfoot lands that had been guaranteed by the Lamed Bull Treaty. The appropriated land gives white ranchers more room to expand.
1880	The official U.S. census lists a scant Blackfoot population of 2,200.
1883	The buffalo, once estimated to number more than 60 million, are all but completely gone from the Plains. Hunting by white people and white ranchers' appropriation of buffalo grazing lands are largely responsible for the buffalos' demise.
1883-1884	The Blackfoot endure what has come to be known as "Starvation Winter." More than 600 Blackfoot die of hunger.
1898	Congress passes the Curtis Act, abolishing the rights of all tribal governments for all Native Americans.
1934	Congress passes the Wheeler-Howard Act, reversing the Curtis Act and allowing Native Americans to reinstitute their tribal governments.
1950s-1960s	Blackfoot culture deteriorates to such a degree that few Blackfoot know or study the tribe's ancestral language, Algonquian.
1970s-1990s	The remaining Blackfoot, realizing they have almost completely lost all traces of their heritage, begin to turn to their surviving elders to learn the stories and traditions of their ancestors. Indian Days celebrations are organized annually in July on Blackfoot reservation lands in Montana.

INDEX